Out and About at the THEATER

by Bitsy Kemper
illustrated by Zachary Trover

Special thanks to our advisers for their expertise:

Michael Lagerquist, Director of Public Relations
Department of Theatre and Dance
Minnesota State University, Mankato

Susan Kesselring, M.A., Literacy Educator
Rosemount–Apple Valley–Eagan (Minnesota) School District

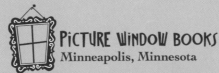

PICTURE WINDOW BOOKS
Minneapolis, Minnesota

To my children, Lucy, Mitch, and Vinny, and to future theatergoers
everywhere: break a leg! –BK

Editor: Nick Healy
Designer: Tracy Kaehler
Page Production: Lori Bye
Creative Director: Keith Griffin
Editorial Director: Carol Jones
The illustrations in this book were created digitally.

Picture Window Books
5115 Excelsior Boulevard
Suite 232
Minneapolis, MN 55416
877-845-8392
www.picturewindowbooks.com

Printed in the United States of America.

Library of Congress Cataloging-in-Publication Data
Kemper, Bitsy.
Out and about at the theater / by Bitsy Kemper ; illustrated by Zachary Trover.
p. cm.
Includes bibliographical references.
ISBN-13: 978-1-4048-2281-8 (hardcover)
ISBN-10: 1-4048-2281-X (hardcover)
1. Theater—Juvenile literature. I. Trover, Zachary. II. Title.
PN2037.K375 2006
792—dc22   2006003559

We're going on a field trip to the theater. We can't wait!

<u>Things to find out:</u>

Where do actors put on their makeup and costumes?

What is the green room?

How do actors know where to stand onstage?

Who is involved in putting on a play?

3

Welcome to the Roxy Theater! My name is Tom. I'm an actor. We put on a different play almost every month at the Roxy.

The performance doesn't start for a while, so I have time to show you around. Have you ever seen a live play before? Today, you will visit places the audience never gets to see.

We'll use the stage door. This is where the actors and crew enter the theater.

Sometimes fans stand outside the stage door after shows. They wait to see the actors leaving. Fans might even get an autograph.

The cast and crew are getting ready to perform. It is opening night for our new musical, and showtime will be here soon.

We actors have to get ready. The crew makes sure our costumes and makeup are just right. Crew members also prepare the scenes onstage, and they set up the lighting. There goes Mitch, our stage manager. He makes sure everything gets done on time.

For every actor onstage, there is at least one more person behind the scenes. These people are called the stage crew. They include the stage manager, lighting team, costume makers, scene builders, and others.

The people who work in our costume shop have a big job. Most plays involve lots of actors and many wardrobe changes. Our costume shop crew has to create all of those costumes.

The costume shop stores many wardrobe pieces to choose from. We might need fancy gowns, space suits, or monkey costumes. If the costume shop doesn't have what we need, the crew will make it. Each costume is tailored to fit the actor.

Actors' names are stitched inside each of their costumes. This helps them know for sure they've got the one that fits just right.

This is where actors put on makeup before going onstage. We have lots of makeup stations, so everyone can find a place to sit. Each station has a mirror surrounded by lightbulbs. The bright light helps actors see exactly what they will look like under the stage lights.

The Roxy also has dressing rooms for men and women. Some theaters have separate dressing rooms for big stars. During the show, actors often hurry to their dressing rooms for wardrobe changes.

During rehearsals, actors who need help with makeup are taught by a professional makeup artist. Then actors apply their own makeup for shows.

11

Once in costume and makeup, actors hang out in the green room. We use it as a waiting room before going onstage. It is best if we stay here when we're not performing. That way, we don't get in the way of the cast and crew who need to be near the stage.

Speakers in the green room let us hear the action onstage. Once the play starts, we listen to the performance. Each actor knows when it is time for him or her to head for the stage.

Most theaters have a room where actors wait to go onstage. It is called the green room, no matter what color the walls are painted. No one knows for sure where the name came from.

13

Now we are in the area known as backstage. Technically, it's not behind the stage, but more on the side of the stage. Sometimes this area is called the wings. From here, we can see and hear everything onstage, but the audience can't see us. This is where I will wait for my cue when the show starts.

A cue is a word, phrase, or action that tells an actor when it's his or her turn to go onstage.

15

Look up, everyone. There is a whole other world over our heads. The area above the stage has to be very tall, so large sets can be raised and lowered from above.

16

There's Hugo on the catwalk. He makes sure lights are aimed at the exact spots where the actors will stand. His lights can make it look like a bright morning for part of the show and a moonlit night at another time. You can also see a speaker hanging nearby. Stage speakers are used for sound effects, like the noise of traffic or birds flying by.

All stage lights use white bulbs. Colored plastic covers called gels are often placed in front of lights. These gels change the color of the beam that shines on the stage.

17

That's Perry, our director. He is placing tape marks on the stage floor. They are called spike marks. These marks help actors remember where to stand during certain parts of the play. Actors have to be in the right place so the lights shine on them perfectly.

Our stage floor also has two sets of trapdoors. There is a hidden room beneath the stage. Actors can use trapdoors to suddenly appear or disappear from stage. Also, the crew can raise and lower parts of the set from below.

Onstage, the lights can be so hot and bright that actors might feel like they need sunscreen.

BOOKMOBILE
101 RAGGED EDGE ROAD SOUTH
CHAMBERSBURG, PA17202

19

Can you hear the orchestra getting ready? Musicians sit in a pit in front of the stage. We want to be sure the audience can see the show, so the pit is lower than the stage.

Our theater has 400 seats. Some theaters seat fewer than 50 people. Others can hold more than 1,000. Seats are arranged so everyone can see all of the actors and sets onstage.

It is time for me to get into costume. While I go backstage, you can take your seats for the show. Thanks for coming to the Roxy Theater.

When actors and crew members say "break a leg," they aren't being mean. In the world of theater, that's a way of wishing someone good luck.

SETTING THE STAGE

What you need:
five chairs and your imagination

What you do:
Pretend you are the director. Rearrange the chairs in different ways, depending on the setting. You'll be amazed at how much you can do with five simple chairs. Create the following settings:

1. a bus or airplane (one chair in front, followed by two rows of two)

2. living room (two together and three together to make a sofa and loveseat, as if in front of a TV)

3. church (all five together to form a pew)

4. classroom (one facing the other four that are in a row, or one facing two rows of two)

5. movie theater (one row of two and one row of three, spaced out)

What other settings can you come up with using these same five chairs? Can you imagine a short play that might take place in one of these settings?

FUN FACTS ·

- Theater has been around for centuries. The ancient Egyptians, Greeks, and Romans were active in performing plays.

- Before electricity was available, theaters were lit by candles—lots and lots of candles.

- The difference between a Broadway show and an off-Broadway show in New York City is the number of seats in the theater, not the address. Broadway shows have 500 seats or more. Off-Broadway shows have fewer than 500 seats.

- In 2005, nearly 12 million people saw Broadway shows. They created $825 million in sales.

- William Shakespeare wrote many of his greatest plays for London's Globe Theater, which opened in 1599. His plays have been performed in theaters for more than 400 years.

- At most live shows, audience members receive programs (called playbills on Broadway). Programs have lots of information about the show, including the names of actors, song lists, and a list of scenes.

GLOSSARY

backstage—the area behind and beside the stage where actors and crew wait out of the audience's view; also called the wings

cast—the actors performing in a show

catwalk—a narrow, hanging walkway; theater lights and speakers are hung from the catwalk

cue—a word or action that signals an actor to go onstage

green room—a waiting room where actors stay, in costume and makeup, before going backstage

set—the stage scene where the action is taking place, such as the kitchen or a mountaintop

showtime—the scheduled time at which a play begins

stage crew—the "behind the curtain" people that help make the play happen, including designers and workers of the set, lighting, and costumes

wardrobe—the costumes actors wear during shows

TO LEARN MORE

At the Library

Aliki. *A Play's the Thing*. New York: HarperCollins, 2005.

Hill, Mary. *Let's Go to a Movie*. New York: Children's Press, 2004.

Miller, Kimberly M. *Backstage at a Play*. New York: Children's Press, 2003.

Wells, Rosemary. *The School Play*. New York: Hyperion Books for Children, 2001.

On the Web

FactHound offers a safe, fun way to find Internet sites related to this book. All of the sites on FactHound have been researched by our staff.

1. Visit *www.facthound.com*
2. Type in this special code for age-appropriate sites: 140482281X
3. Click on the FETCH IT button.

Your trusty FactHound will fetch the best sites for you!

INDEX

Look for all the books in the Field Trips series:

Out and About at ...

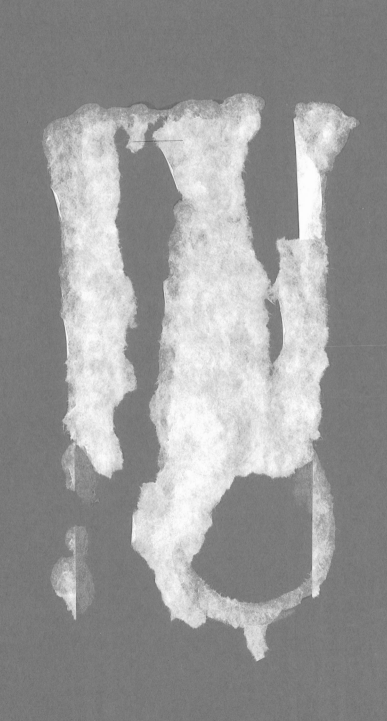